Amelia's Adventures

THE HOLIDAY FAIRY'S ENCHANTED QUEST

By Amelia & Marge Di Blasio

I0519398

Illustrated by Ishara Jayasinghe | Formatted by Ell Om

ISBN: 978-1-998158-28-7 (Paperback)

www.margediblasio.org/books

To all our fantastic readers,
young and grown-up, this book is dedicated to you!
Keep dreaming, keep creating, and keep spreading
the holiday magic all year long.

One frosty morning, in a cute little snowy village, surrounded by tall pine trees, there lived a curious and cheerful girl named Amelia. She loved going on adventures in the snowy wonderland right outside her front door.

She couldn't wait for the holiday season because she knew it meant one thing: presents! Her eyes lit up with excitement as she imagined about all the wonderful toys she'd soon be unwrapping.

As Amelia dreamed about her holiday surprises, she began her exciting journey. While walking in the snow, something unusual caught her eye. She spotted a tiny and enchanting creature with delicate, snowy-white wings.

"Hi there, I'm Snow Sparkle, the holiday snow fairy!"

Amelia's eyes lit up with excitement. "Wow, a real holiday fairy? Can you help me get more presents?"

Snow Sparkle giggled and said, "Oh, I'm here to help you discover something more wonderful Amelia!"

Amelia replied, "Oh, Snow Sparkle! I can't wait for all the gifts I'll get. What could possibly be more amazing than presents?"

Just then, Snow Sparkle waved her tiny wand and whisked Amelia away to another place. It was a place where there weren't a lot of holiday gifts.

Amelia asked, "Whoa, where are we?"

The fairy smiled and replied, "We're here to explore a different world. Take a look around!"

As Amelia and Snow Sparkle continued their quest, Amelia's sharp eyes spotted a little girl. She sat by the side of a building, wearing tattered, worn-out clothes that were far too big for her tiny frame. She looked like she needed help.

Curious, Amelia turned to Snow Sparkle and asked, "Why does that girl look so sad? Does she need more toys?"

Snow Sparkle explained, "That little girl's name is Sophie. Her parents are sick and unable to work so she stays with her grandma who is quite old. They haven't had food for several days. She washes cars in the morning, but it isn't enough to support everybody. At night, she asks people for food and hopes that someone kind will give her money.

Toys can bring her a temporary smile, but what she really needs is a kind act that can make a difference for her family."

Later, Amelia watched as a man gave Sophie some food. Sophie's face lit up with joy, and she ran to share it with her grandma.

Amelia discovered that in Sophie's world, some people didn't have enough food and had to ask for help. In the spirit of kindness, they came together to support one another.

Snow Sparkle whispered, "Amelia, receiving presents is a lot of fun, but there's something more magical about giving. It's about sharing joy, kindness, and love. This will make your heart sparkle even brighter than a Christmas tree."

Seeing the joy on Sophie's face when she received help filled Amelia's heart with warmth. She realized, that even though she was excited about her holiday toys, not everyone was as fortunate as she was. She knew there was something wonderful she could do.

From that magical day on, Amelia discovered the incredible power and joy of giving. While she still loved her toys and presents, she realized that even the smallest acts of kindness could create massive happiness for others.

Now, when the holidays draw near, Amelia sprinkles kindness, joy and love, like fairy dust, ready to make the world a little brighter for everyone. She discovered that this is the most enchanting and empowering wonder of all during the holiday season!

Other Recommended Books

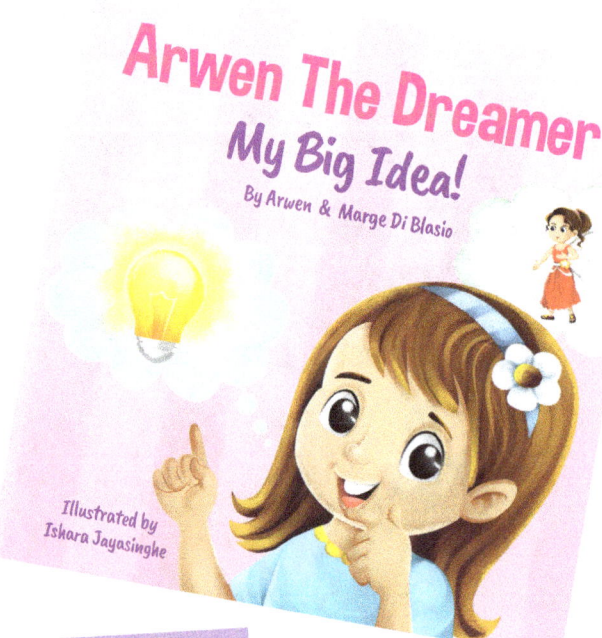

About the Authors

AMELIA DI BLASIO is a young adventurer who loves hanging out with friends and going on awesome journeys. She enjoys dancing, reading, painting, swimming, and, best of all, having a blast!

This book marks her second adventure in writing, following the heartwarming "Mommy, Please Spend Time with Me," co-authored with her mom at the age of 6, as part of her delightful creative project.

MARGE CASTILLON DI BLASIO lives in Canada, where it can get super chilly. So, when the cold weather rolls in, she and her kids love to take on creative challenges. She's a big fan of reading exciting stories, staying active, going on adventures, and hanging out with her family. She wrote this book to have a super creative adventure with her daughter, Amelia.
It's all about fun and creativity rolled into one!

www.ingramcontent.com/pod-product-compliance
Lightning Source LLC
Chambersburg PA
CBHW081014120626

46546CB00010B/3141